WHY THIS, WHY ME, AND WHY NOW?

Keys for Survival in Perilous Times That Will Help You to Understand God's Will for Your Life as You Face Daily Challenges

Cynthia Finklea

ISBN 978-1-63903-720-9 (paperback)
ISBN 978-1-63903-721-6 (digital)

Christian Faith Publishing, Inc.
832 Park Avenue
Meadville, PA 16335
www.christianfaithpublishing.com

Printed in the United States of America

CONTENTS

INTRODUCTION

As you read this book, my prayer for you is that you will have a deeper measure and a higher level of God's love and His revelation for you through the life of David. David, God's chosen shepherd boy who later was anointed God's chosen king. God's revelation of David was revealed to man when David was a boy and not when David became king. God's purpose and plans for your life started from the very beginning; before you were born, God knew you. His revelation, gifts, and the promises for your life are there, you need to walk in them. Believe that you are who God's says you are and not what man says about you. You are even more gifted than you think you are. God has already fixed you for the shoes He made for you to walk in. You need to believe and trust in the fact that God Almighty has already paved the way for your life. As He did for David and others, He will do it for you. But there is a price to pay for the anointing that's on your life. The road is not easy, the journey will get tough along the way, you need to stay focus and faithful to God. When you do this, you can face any valleys and climb any mountain that's before you. Just as God did it for David, He will do the same for you. You need to know how to navigate through life's challenges, knowing that you are a winner. David knew he was a winner when he faced Goliath, but when he faced Saul, this event played out differently. Regardless as to how things are revealed, you need to keep your focus on God and never magnify the matter that is before you. Whether your lenses are adjusted or not, make the adjustment; keep your eyes on the Lord, even if it is difficult for you to see what He is doing. The enemy always wants you to lose contact with God. Once you do, he has accomplished his goal: failure. Because he failed at what he was appointed to do, he wants you to fail also. Failure is never an option with God. If your eyes have wondered, get them back where they belong: on God. He alone can solve any problem. God wants and has the very best in store for your life.

In this study, you will be able to see and know without a shadow of doubt God's directions and destiny for this season of your life, especially how and where God wants you to stand.

You will be able to know Genesis 18:14, "Is there anything too hard for the Lord?" David knew there was not anything too hard for God. Do you?

You will also see that not only did Moses, Joshua, and other faithful men and women of God knew God as their Deliver but David knew God as his only Deliverer.

All of us have a position description, whether we recognize it or not. It is when we fail to recognize God as our leader that we find ourselves in trouble, headed in the wrong direction. You may know someone who is exceptionally smart, gifted at what they do. There are individuals who are gifted but arrogant with their gift. We need to all remind ourselves that it is nothing we have done to make ourselves smart. Yes, you may have studied, but in the end, it was God's gift to you. God wants us to share our gifts with others in a godly manner and not belittling others because of their skills. Regardless of your gift, it is important to God. Each of us was divinely crafted by the Hand of God. So let's get started!

If you have set your sail, make sure you are sailing in God's direction. If you have not set sail, go ahead and start your engine. Check the gauge, you do not want to rush. Rushing through this course will cause you to miss what God wants you to see so you will know how to navigate through whatever lies ahead. You will be able to recognize what to do when you run into roadblocks, detours, and bumps along the way. David did not allow none of the bumps and bruises along the way to prevent him from fulfilling God's purpose and promises for his life. The journey may be long, but look at what you will gain for going the distance with God instead of getting a quick fix. God wants to build strength in your life. Being strong in the Lord will cause you to be able to sustain any wind that blows against you. Any waters that tries to drown you.

Because of the season we are in, God is raising up warriors. Warriors who will fight in the Spirit and not in the flesh. Warriors who will seek His face in times that are good and times that are bad.

The choices we make will reveal the depth of our hearts.

David knew who, what, when and how to fight. He knew that fighting Goliath was his purpose but fighting Saul was not. There was a showdown between Goliath and David. David, the young man that he was, was called to this battle. Even in the midst of this battle, David knew that Goliath was already a defeated foe. Yet David still relied on and trusted in God. We need to remind ourselves that even when we feel strong and well able, the key to survival is to lean on God and not ourselves. Have you ever seen someone who handled a matter, but immediately afterward, they stumble and fall? Could it be they got out of leaning on God and started leaning on their own strength?

Question:
What is your purpose in the matter?

CHAPTER 1

Who Am I, Lord?

From the beginning of time, man has always questioned who God says he is. In Genesis 1, God made man, set man in the Garden of Eden, and gave him authority over the fish of the sea, over the birds of the sky, and over the animals that crawled upon the land. We know the story: Adam failed to obey one of the most important thing God asked of him. Both Adam and Eve ate from the Tree of the Knowledge of Good and Evil. Because of their disobedience, Adam and Eve saw the nakedness of their bodies. God's response to our disobedience will bring correction, healing, and restoration if we will accept God's hand in the matter. Restoration comes in many forms. It is up to us to receive how God chooses to restore our brokenness. Look at God's response to Adam and Eve, He asked them a question, a very important question. Adam and Eve was hiding from God in the Garden of Eden. The Lord God called Adam, "Where are you?"

Adam said, "I hid from you because I was naked."

God said, "Who told you, you were naked?"

Isn't this how we are today? To some degree, we are hiding from God because we do not know who we are.

God said, "I didn't tell you that you were naked. I knew you fell, I clothed you so others could not see your nakedness."

God will take what was wrong and make it right.

When God wants to demonstrate Himself mighty in your life and in the lives of others, He will do or ask something that's beyond what man can think or do. When God was ready to deliver the children of Israel out of Egypt, God called Moses, a man who could barely speak. One who murdered an Egyptian. What was Moses's response to God? "Who am I to appear before Pharaoh?" Moses was looking at his fouls and failures. With God, He sees us as the apple of His eyes. Even though we disappoint God from time to time, we are still His children and He loves us.

When you know who you are, you will speak to kings and not be afraid! Moses was given a task that was assigned by God. What have you been given?

Fear will always cause you to stumble in the place God called you.

When facing the most difficult time in our lives, it is then we see and know who we are. It reveals our God, His love for us, and how we choose to walk with Him.

There are some things we need to know and things we need to consider for the journey.

1. WHO IS YOUR GOD?
    From Genesis to Revelation, God reveals Himself to man. In the Book of Psalm, David opened his heart to us with his expressions of who God is and the faithfulness of our God. As you move forward in life, you cannot just read about God, you will come to a point that you will either accept or reject who God says He is. What I found interesting about the life of David is that no matter what David did, the good, bad, and the ugly, David never lost his respect and love for God. In this book, you will see David's strengths and weaknesses as well as David's knowledge of God. David knew where to lean, David leaned on God.

    David declares "I love you Lord: you are my strength. The Lord is my rock, my fortress, and my Savior; My God is my rock, in whom I find protection. He is my shield, the power that saves me and my place of safety. I called on the Lord, who is worthy of praise, and He saved me from my enemies." (Psalm 18:1–3 NLT)

If you do not know the God of Abraham, Isaac, and Jacob, you will lose out on life. Your life will never be what God intended for you. He is the Almighty God. Yes, He can do anything. Genesis 18:14 asks a very powerful question: "Is there anything too hard for God?" The answer will always be no, there is nothing too hard for our God. If you have not made Jesus Christ the Lord of your life, ask Him to come into your heart. You need to make Jesus your Lord and Savior today! Read Romans 10:9, the message is clear. When you make Jesus Christ the Lord of your life, you will no longer be under the authority of the enemy but a child of the Most High God. Jesus told us in this life, we will have trials and tribulations. But we are to be of good cheer because He (Jesus) has already defeated whatever we will face. Being a child of God and knowing what His word says will cause you to stand when everything around you is falling apart. Why? Because you know what God has declared over you.

"Do not be afraid, for I have ransomed you. I have called you by name, you are mine. When you go through deep waters, I will be with you. When you go through the rivers of difficulty, you will not drown. When you walk through fire of oppression, you will not be burned up; the flames will not consume you. For I am the Lord, your God, the Holy One of Israel, your Savior" (Isaiah 43:1 NLT).

"I, yes I am the Lord, and there is no other Savior" (Isaiah 43:11 NLT).

"From eternity to eternity I am God. No one can snatch anyone out of my hand. No can undo what I have done" (Isaiah 43:13 NLT).

When God gets ready to do something in your life, you will know it. You may not understand it, but if you will look and listen, you can see how God is revealing Himself to you during this particular season. When it looks like God is silent, He is not. Whatever needs to happen has happened. God has already finished the work, we just need to rest in the assurance of who our God is. Stand, you will see the salvation of the Lord.

2.   WHAT IS MY TEST IN THIS MESS?

Saul and all the men of Israel was in a mess. There was a giant threat against them and his name was Goliath. King Saul and his men were greatly afraid (1 Samuel 17:11).

David's father sent him to take food to his brothers while they were on the battlefield. David's oldest brother, Eliab, questioned why David was there. 1 Samuel 17 (NKJ) said, "Why did you come here? And with whom have you left those few sheep in the wilderness? I know your pride and the insolence of your heart, for you have come down to see the battle?" There is so much we can learn from this.

Notice, this is David oldest brother, Eliab, addressing him. He was the first one passed over when Samuel came to anoint a king over Israel. Eliab's anger aroused against David. He had an inner issue with David. An inward anger is just as worst as an outer display of anger. It is living and growing inside of you that others cannot see until something causes you to reveal the nature of your response in a matter. This is the reason why God says in James 1:20 (NLT), "Human anger does not produce the righteousness God desires." Eliab had something in his heart working against his younger brother, David. I believe that anger was an outer display of jealous in Eliab's heart toward David. Being jealous of what God has predestined for someone will destroy you.

What can we learn from what Eliab said to David?

"Why did you come down here?"

Here you see Eliab questioning David's reason for being there. This sounds like David's presence once again overshadowing Eliab as it did when David was anointed king and Eliab was not. Know that it does not matter what anyone says about you. When God has called and equip you, no man can stop the promises of God for your life.

"And with whom have you left those few sheep in the wilderness?"

Eliab was belittling David's responsibility as a shepherd boy. You only have a few (meaning your task is small) sheep to watch. Why are you here? Isn't this like some of the situations we face on a daily basis? Why did you get the job and I didn't? Why did you get the spouse you wanted and all I got was divorce papers. It does not matter what it is, it's just the why you and not me?

"I know your pride and the insolence of your heart, for you have come down to see the battle."

Eliab wanted his words to shut David down, they did not. Man will do or say anything to attempt to destroy what God has called you to do. Never allow man's word to override God's plans for your life.

If you hear yourself saying why them and not me, know that God has a plan further greater than your eyes can see. When things are not going the way you think they should, continue to take God at His Word. David was a boy when Samuel anointed him as king. David did not begin his reign as king until he was thirty years old (2 Samuel 5:4). David did not allow any of the bumps and bruises along the way prevent him from fulfilling God's purpose and promises for his like. What about you?

Life is like a jigsaw puzzle. The picture is not complete until all the pieces are framed and fitted together in their proper place. Framed, because there is a particular way God wants your scattered pieces to look. Fitted, because God will not allow you to force together what He has not put together. God's way will cause it to automatically fit even when we face challenges along the way. In the end, it will all work out for our good. The picture will be crystal clear. You may not like what you see, but look at it through the eyes of God and from His Word. Doing things your way will cause you to force scattered pieces together. When we force or make something happen that was not framed by God, it will change the course of our lives and cause us more pain and disappointment than we could ever imagine. Forcing it never makes a proper fit. There is always pain in forcing something to happen. We know this: it is like wearing a pair of shoes that does not fit, they hurt. This is why it is important that we allow God to take all the scattered pieces of our lives and fit them together.

At some point in life, if you have not already asked yourself, you need to ask yourself, "Who am I?"

David knew who he was, his hope and confidence was in God who made him the man he was.

When David watched over his father's flock, he knew and conducted himself as a shepherd boy. As a boy, David knew the importance of his responsibility not only to his father but to the sheep he guarded.

When it was time to anoint David as king, he did not hide like as Saul did. When Samuel came to anoint Saul as king, Saul hid from Samuel.

When you know who you are, you can conquer anything. David knew who he was, he remained anchored in the Lord his God. It does not matter who you are or where you come from, there will always be someone or something you have to contend with.

Oppression will often cause you to question those around you who God has placed in your life. In the Gospel of John, you see John the Baptist declaring who Jesus is, the Lamb of God that takes away the sins of the world. While in prison (under stress and oppression), John the Baptist sent his disciples to Jesus to ask Him, are you the Messiah or should we look for someone else? If we allow opposition of this world get to us, it can cause the fire around us to burn so bright that our eyes only see the ashes and not the beauty of what God has set before us.

David never allowed the fire that was burning in his life cause him not to see the glory of God and what God was doing while on the run from Saul. David always declared himself as a servant of Saul. Even in the midst of the storm, David never lost sight of who Saul was, God's anointed. It is one of the most important tools for fighting any battle. Until you recognize and understand God's purpose in your life and for your life, you will never comprehend the depth and wealth of who you really are.

Question:
Are you ready to walk in who God says you are?

CHAPTER 2

That Person

In life, we all have someone or something that we can look at and say "that person" or "that thing" has brought me or is taking me to the place God has destined for my life. It is up to you whether or not you recognize "that person."

Remember, all twelve disciples were invited to the table. Men with scattered dreams, broken pieces, but they all came to the table.

In this book, you will see how David was guided by:

1. God
2. Samuel
3. Saul
4. Jonathan
5. Abigail
6. Nathan
7. Absalom

Samuel was a "that person" in the life of Saul and David. Samuel was able to walk with Saul and David even in their disobedience to God. Saul completely disobeyed God. David honored and loved God, but David also struggled in the area of disobedience.

God raised up Samuel to serve Him and His people, the children of Israel. But Saul did not realize Samuel's leadership in his life. When we recognize the reason and the purpose for that person in our lives, we will see what God see and do what God wants us to do. It is like looking at front of a jigsaw puzzle box. The picture is clear, all of the pieces are glued together. No lines or missing pieces, you see the complete picture of what is inside the box. When you open the box, you see all the scattered pieces, everything looks broken and torn apart. This is how we sometimes view our lives, this is not how God sees us. Until we give God all the scattered pieces of our lives and allow Him to fix them, we will continue to live in our brokenness with hearts that are damaged and crushed into pieces. Hidden in boxes until we allow the cover to be move. God has given and appointed someone in different seasons of our lives to walk with us through the good and the bad. The problem is when we want to decide who we will walk with and how we will walk with them.

Even though the appointment of Saul grieved Samuel, Samuel obeyed God's commission. Samuel recognized that Saul was "that person" for this season in the history of God's people. Jesus did the same with Judas. Jesus knew the heart and purpose Judas played in His life. Jesus could have easily destroyed Judas, but He did not. Instead, Jesus told Judas in John 13:27 (NKJV), "What you do, do quickly." Jesus was able to say this because He knew Judas was "that person" in His life. God choose Saul to be a "that person" in the lives of the Children of Israel because of the desires of their hearts.

Saul was unable to successfully complete his assignment because:

Saul never acknowledged who God said he was (1 Samuel 9:20–21).

When Samuel presented Saul to the People of Israel, "Saul hid among the baggage" (1 Samuel 10:22).

Saul was insecure. He never recognized the importance of obeying God. This is clearly a trap that the enemy sets in our lives. The enemy never wants us to focus on what God says. Three of Saul's major failure were:

1. Saul sacrificed the burnt offering.
   When God wanted to settle an account with the Amalekites, Saul did not complete the mission. Saul was instructed to kill the entire Amalekite nation, man and female and all of their animals. Saul and his men spared what seemed right in their eyes.

God gave Samuel to Saul to guide and instruct him in the things he needed to do. Saul was more concerned about fulfilling his own lustful desires that he failed miserably at the things of God.

2. Saul was emotionally unstable.
    Our character reveals who we are. Life is full of many choices, we should govern ourselves by the Word of God.
    "Guard your heart above all else, for it determines the course of your life" (Proverbs 4:23 NLT).

Along life's journey, you will encounter unknowns. It is how you handle them that will determine your future. The steps of a righteous man is ordered by the Lord, He will place unfamiliar people or things in our path to help guide us along the way. We must be careful how we handle them, for they can change the course we are traveling on.

3. Saul was more concerned about what man said than what God said. In 1 Samuel 15:23 (NLT), "Then Saul admitted to Samuel, 'Yes, I have sinned. I have disobeyed your instructions and the Lord's command, for I was afraid of the people and did what they demanded.'"

Question:
What are you going to do with "that person" in your life?

CHAPTER 3

What Are You Holding?

Our hands can be used to perform many functions. It is up to you how, when, and where you use them. You will see and discover how Samuel, Saul, and David respond to some of the challenges that was handed to them and what was placed in their hands.

With Samuel, he learned God's plan for his life at an early age. While serving Eli the Priest of God, it was here where Samuel learned the voice of God. Eli instructs Samuel, "the voice you are hearing is not my voice but the voice of God. When you hear it again, this is what you need to say 'Speak Lord, your servant is listening.'"

Hearing, listening, and obeying are three powerful weapons given to us by God, but we sometimes overlook the effectiveness of them. Yes, it is vital that we operate out of our spirit, but it is just as important that we filter these three elements through the Word of God. What is God saying to us and are we listening and obeying Him?

What did Samuel, the prophet of God, hold in his hands?

The Children of Israel: When Samuel appointed his sons as judges over Israel, the Elders' response was "we want a king to judge us," not your sons. Because their request displeased Samuel, he sought the Lord for guidance. Samuel filtered his pain of rejection through the hand of God. God reminded Samuel to "heed the voice of the people in all that they say, for they have not rejected you, but they have rejected me that I should not reign over them." Notice how Samuel handled their response. Even though Samuel saw it as a rejection of his decision to set his sons over them, Samuel released it to God. Samuel handed what was handed to him to God.

It is extremely important that the thing we hold close to us can bring us to a place of healing and deliverance if we give it to God. Out of obedience, Samuel warned the people of what would happen because they asked for a king to lead them.

Samuel also held Saul and David in his hands. Both men were anointed by God as king over Israel. Saul walked in disobedience to God. On the other hand, we see David, the shepherd boy, was obedient to God. Were there times when David fall in life, yes? But it wasn't the fall that kept David from God, it was David's heart for God that kept him close to God. The power in this was the fact that Samuel was able to balance his hands and serve both kings. There are times when God will give you one thing to handle and you need to handle it to the best of knowledge. But there are also times when God will give you multiple things such as he did with Samuel. When this happens, don't feel overwhelmed. Remember, God knows exactly what He is doing and why He has chosen to you carry out this mission. So prepare yourself, wash your hands and always be ready for the call.

How did Saul hold Jonathan, Israel, and David in his hands? In looking at some of the events of Saul's life, you can see that Saul was not one who stood up to the challenges before him. Saul failed to be the father he needed to be for Jonathan. Jonathan demonstrated great love and compassion for his father until it was revealed to him the true nature of Saul's heart toward David. How can it be that the king did not realize David in his life but the son did? Because the king was more concerned about how he looked to man than how he looked to God. Jonathan's heart was committed to God more than his commitment to his father, King Saul. There will come a time in your life when you will have to make a choice, a choice that seems to others that it is the wrong step that you are taking. But if you will keep your hand in God's hands, you will win every time, no matter who it is that is opposing what's in your hand. Your obedience and faithfulness for God will see you through anything!

Even though our parents may fail us, God will never fail us. He is always there whether you can see His hands or not. God is there leading and guiding you every step of the way. You need to hold on to Him and never let go.

After David recognized Jonathan's faithfulness to do the right thing no matter what, David was able to draw from Jonathan's wisdom to get away from the hands of Saul.

Obeying and disobeying God's instruction is key to the survival of your future. Saul's disobedience to wait on the Prophet Samuel forever changed God's direction for Saul's life. Saul focused more on the troops than waiting on Samuel to offer the burnt offering unto the Lord. Saul stepped out of his shoes into another man's shoes. Wow, how many times have we done this? Because Saul took on Samuel's role, Samuel informs Saul that your kingdom must end, the Lord has already sought another to be king over Israel. If you find yourself stepping in someone else's shoes, then step out of them. It is easier to step out of something than to be pulled out.

Saul gets another opportunity to show his obedience to God. But he fails again. This time, it is Samuel who took what was in Saul's hand to do and completed the assignment by killing Agag, king of the Amalekites. If only Saul would have been more concerned about his loyalty to God than the thoughts and ways of man, his life would have given honor to God and the people he was chosen to serve.

At the beginning of Saul's reign, he wasn't concerned about what man thoughts of him. When Samuel presented Saul to the people in 1 Samuel 10:25–27, there were men whose hearts supported Saul. There were also men who complained against Saul, but Saul ignored them. How can a man start out as gifted as Saul was, one who ignored the words of man to later becoming a man who accepted the words of man over the words of God?

Faith in God is not only trusting God, faith in God requires a believer to listen and obey God's instructions.

Let's look at what happened to David prior to the death of Goliath. David, shepherd boy trained in the field, cared for and provided protection for this father's flock. David's father handed him the responsibility of caring for the family's inheritance. Why did David's father give him this task considering David was his youngest son? Could it be that David's father saw something in David that he did not see in his other sons? We should be more like David, a young boy, given a big responsibility, but yet he did what was handed of him instead of complaining. Why me?

If you find yourself complaining or questioning something that was handed to you, then tell yourself, "I can do this." I believe you can! You just need to believe in yourself. Stop looking at what you see. If you continue to look at what is going on around you, you will never get to the place God has handpicked just for you. Besides, it is easy to look at the wrong thing. When looking at the wrong thing, it will cause you to go in the wrong direction. Put your focus on God and allow His Spirit to live in you. When you do this, you can conquer His goals for your life. His goals are far better than the gold of this world.

When God gives you something, it is in your life for a reason and not necessarily for a season. Only God knows your tomorrows. God knew David would one day need to know how to care for His sheep, the children of Israel.

David anointed king. Samuel anoints David as God's chosen king. God commissioned Samuel to place the children of Israel leadership in David's hand.

On this journey, God will send someone or something to you to prepare you for what He has destined for your life. I am sure David meditated on this event, "me a shepherd being anointed as king." What was so powerful about David's life at this point was the fact that David continue to do what he knew to do, serve his father in the fields. David did not change his pattern of life until the appointed time. What we sometimes fail to do in our place of preparation is to continue to do what we are already doing. Do not change lanes until God reveals the appointed time for you to move. Remember, Saul was still king. David did not move out of his position until he instructed to do so. In 1 Samuel 17, David's father Jesse send him to take provisions to his brothers who were on the battlefield with Saul's Army. While there, David heard about the cause that came up against Saul's army named Goliath. David was not afraid of the giant that stood before them. As people, we sometimes run from the fight because we do not recognize that the training ground is our battleground. Where you are trained is where you learn if you will listen and obey what God is telling you.

What is the ugly cause that has raised its head up against you?

If you are afraid of the mountain that is before you, don't be. Listen to David's response in 1 Samuel 17:32 (NLT), "Don't worry about this Philistine, I'll go fight him!" You are called and equipped to stand in the place God has prepared just for you. David comprehended and understood the ways of God through His Word. The Word of God will always see through any difficulties you may face.

There will always be someone who wants you to stand in their place, you should stand where God has called you...it's in this place you are trained.

Eliab's attack against David. Eliab, David's oldest brother, opposed what God placed in David's hands to do. Even in the face of opposition, you must stand. Attacks are a part of life. They are there for a reason, the choice is up to you how you allow these attacks to affect you. Attacks from the outside hurts, but when you are attacked from within the camp, that is when the attack is the strongest. Looking at your life, you may be able to say, "I know what it is like to be hit by friendly fire." David's response to Eliab did not move him from the cause that was before them. David kept on moving toward the importance of the matter before him, Goliath. Why? Because what was stirring in Eliab's heart was not as important than what was stirring in David's heart. Staying focus will allow you to properly handle that that's in your hand when someone else heart is contaminated. David did not ignore the pain in his brother's heart, but the key to this situation was David's response. David declared to Goliath in 1 Samuel 17:47 (NLT), "This is the Lord's battle, and He will give you to us!" At the end of this battle, it was Goliath's head in David's hand.

Now the nine-foot giant is no longer a threat to God's people.

Is what you holding, holding you or are you holding it?

Question
Have you slain your giant?

CHAPTER 4

Overcoming Setbacks

Setbacks comes in many ways. They come through disappointments, bitterness, jealousy, hardship, this list can go on and on. No matter how the attacks come, we should never lose our hope in God. God is standing with us ready to help, heal and care for us. Hebrews 13:5 (AMP) said, "I will not in any way fail you nor give you up nor leave you without support. I will not in any degree leave you helpless nor forsake nor let you down (relax My hold on you)! Assuredly not!"

The Lord said in Psalm 91:14 (NLT) "I will rescue those who love me. I will protect those who trust in my name."

David understood God's divine purpose for his life. You need to realize that no man can change the fingerprint God has for you. Man can surgically remove your fingerprint from your hand, but God wants man to know that your true identity lies in who He created you to be. We can change the outside, but it's the inside God wants to change.

Look at how David use his experiences, the good and the bad, as he navigated through life's journey.

In 1 Samuel 26, David knew he did nothing wrong toward King Saul. David was willing to accept Saul's attacks against him could have been instructed by the hand of God. If so, David was willing to make an offering to repent of any transgression he may have committed.

In the thick of the battle, it does not matter who is right or who is wrong. The issue is, will you submit to the hand of God? Many battles that were lost could have been won if only we would kept our eyes fixed on the Lord and watch out for attacks within the camp. Even within your circle, you need to stay on guard. There will always be someone in your camp that God has assigned to you to keep you in check. Don't fight against them, they are there for an important reason of your life. In 1 Samuel 26:1–12 while Saul and his men were camped out one night, David and Abishai found them asleep. Abishai instructed David, "Surely God has handed your enemy over to you. With one stroke I can kill him." David's response was no! You cannot remain innocent if you kill the Lord's anointed.

Let's examine this closely. Saul had three thousand of his elite warriors with him in the wilderness looking for David. Their goal was to kill David. At night to secure their king, the warriors formed a circle around Saul for his safety. David was able to get through the circle because God placed a deep sleep on the soldiers (1 Samuel 26:12). This says a lot. Instead of Saul finding David, David found Saul and his troops sleeping. They were helpless. David could have killed Saul, but he didn't. David had already determined in his heart that he would not touch the Lord's anointed. A determined heart established in the Word of God will guide you in the right direction when you can't guide yourself. David respected Saul as Israel's king. This is where many of our battles are won. It is not at the end where battles are won, it is at the beginning where discussions are made. The enemy wants you to acknowledge the problem before the promise. He wants you to think the problem is bigger than the promises from God. Our enemy is full of lies; God calls him the father of lies.

No matter what the enemy has, he cannot destroy you. Always keep an event that happen in the Bible in your heart, it will sustain you in your times of trouble. If you are not familiar with the life of Job, read it. Job lost much, but his gain was so much greater. I am not speaking of the loss of his children and his procession though they were great losses, Job gained much knowledge and understanding in what really lived in his heart. The enemy's goal is to get you focusing on what happen, this is what Job did. When Job finally released the pain of his loss into the hands of God, Job was able to come to the place of understanding that "though He slay me, yet will I trust

Him." In our deepest place of pain, it is here where we rest in the midst of the storm, in the palm of God's hands. This is a place where David found his comfort, his peace, and his ability to walk through anything that confronted him. Psalm 91:1–2 (KJV) declares, "He that dwelleth in the secret place of the most High shall abide under the shadow of the Almighty. I will say of the Lord, He is my refuge and my fortress: my God in Him will I trust."

We often lose our way, forgetting that God has already made a way. The enemy likes to play tricks on you, causing you to stumble along the way. Allowing you to see the bumps and bruises instead of recognizing the Presence of God. He will present a problem to you in such a way that causes you from seeing God leading you through the problem to promise. When faced with a difficult situation, I remember my momma (my grandmother who raised me). I can still see her at the foot of our bed praying. She loved to whistle and sing, though her voice wasn't pleasant to man, it was to God. If you looked at her in the natural, you could not see what God was doing in her heart. Every day, she wore an apron. Whether she was working at home or cooking and cleaning someone house, she always had her apron on. Why? To me, she was dressed for service. This has helped me so much on my journey. What we tend to view as something simple and small, it usually is big in the eyes of God. What is our assignment and how are we dressed for it?

And when I think about the children of Israel and how they cried out to God and He heard them and He delivered them, something powerful overwhelms my spirit that I can pray from a position in God that brings such healing to my heart. The events of how the Lord delivered the Children of Israel out of slavery has always been a major part of my survival kit, something hidden in my heart forever that carry me during turbulence times. Remember the promise God made to Abraham, how the children of Israel would be in bondage for four hundred years, but He will lead them out of bondage. And He did. Even though God promises are there, life is full of uncertainties, but don't be afraid. God is always there with us whether we can see Him or not, He is there!

I believe the greatest love story ever told is the event that happen in the book of Genesis, how God cared for Adam and Eve during the Fall in the Garden. If viewed through your natural eyes, you will miss God's faithfulness to us when we fall. If you view this through the Spirit, you will see that even when Adam faced his greatest setback, there was God. There are consequences when we sin against God. God covered Adam and Eve's nakedness, set them out of the Garden, so that they would not eat from the Tree of Life and live in sin forever. Now that's love. Stop fighting against what God has already established and ordained for your life. If you are facing a setback, walk it out. Someone once told me that there is nothing that has happen or can happen to you that has not filter through the hand of God.

What looked like a setback for David turned out to be a blessing. With three thousand soldiers chasing after David, he was able to avoid the roadblock Saul had planned for him, God placed them into David's hand.

Do not be discouraged when you see or hear of a roadblock, they are there to reveal the decisions you will make. Will you follow God's way of doing things or will you make your own path in the wilderness?

It breaks our hearts to read about one of David's biggest setback in is life, his affair with Bathsheba. You cannot study the life of David without looking at David's response to God's hand in the matter. When Nathan the Prophet appeared before King David to address what he had done, listen to David's response in 2 Samuel 12:13, "I have sinned against the Lord." From the death of the child born to David and Bathsheba, you can see David operating in a different manner than before. David moved from being a fierce warrior, a man with a sword in his hand to a man who holds much grace in his heart. We will study more about this in chapter 6. What David did was wrong, the affair and the ordering of Uriah's death. And no, God was not going to allow David to move forward without addressing this matter.

Let's examine what David did after Nathan reveals God's response? In 2 Samuel 12:20 (NLT):

1. David got up.

   In facing a setback, if you are knocked down, get up! No matter what you face, when the matter is settled and the results are not what you expect, continue to stand. Do not stay in that place of pain, soaking over the results. Remain faithful to God. Trust Him with your failures, even if you are not the person that caused the pain.

2. David washed himself and put on clothes.

   David cleansed the outside, the washing of his body with his hands. God cleansed the inside when David acknowledged that he sinned against the Lord. When we make mistakes, our hearts are disobedient to God, our final response should always cause us to run to God.

   Knowing the events of Adams and David's life, you can see the importance of omitting where you are to God even though God already knows your position. Adam failed to accept the fact the He was disobedient to God. Whereas David admitted his transgression. A man after God's heart will always cry out to God in times of trouble and peace.

   When the disciples were in the boat, a storm arose, they cried out to Jesus. Jesus calmed the storm. It was Peter who took it another step further. Peter not only wanted to be saved by Jesus, he also wanted to go to Jesus. Peter's heart not only wanted God's hand for deliverance, he also wanted God's presence.

3. And David changed his clothes.

   What you face and your response to it is always a matter of the heart. How you care for your outer body reveals the condition of your heart.

4. David went to the Tabernacle and worshiped the Lord. After that, he returned to the palace and was served food and ate. When our prayers are not answer, the way we think they should, this is when our true relationship with God is

revealed. When God's decision is painful to bear, this is when we need to show our faithfulness to God.

Life's journey is full of many things we will see and experience along the way. God's Word, the Holy Bible, is His gift to us to read, study His ways and guidance for our lives. Submitting to God's hand will cause the anointing, the power of His Word to flow mighty through our lives which brings strength, healing, and protection for our daily responsibilities.

God has provided roadside assistance along the way. Just as there are signs along the road to guide you as you travel, there is God.

For years, I traveled back and forth to work on two major interstates in South Carolina. I saw things I would have never thought I would have seen in my lifetime. Many of the things I saw helped, strengthened, and encouraged me. Road signs are given to instruct us as to how we should travel. Speed limits are given for each road. Why? Because the conditions and circumstances for each road are different, we need to make adjustments when it is needed. This is how life is for every road we travel, there is a certain speed limit we need to obey. Mistakes will happen, it's how we correct them that determines the outcome. When we travel faster than the required speed limit, it open doors for things to happen in our lives. I must confess, I did not always obey the speed limit. There is a sign on an exit that say sharp curve, speed limit 25 mph. At least once or twice a month, there was a vehicle turned over in the curve. When we fail to obey instructions given to us, we can crush and burn. Specific instructions were given, but the driver failed to follow them. Don't crush and burn trying to do something you was not call (instructed) to do. Even when your set back is at your own hands, God's promise is that He will see you through whatever is thrown at you.

David was thrown a curve ball when he went from the palace of the king into a cave on the run from Saul. Life's setbacks can hit you at any moment, anytime, day, or night. Being prepared will give you the advantage of operating ahead than behind. A wise navigator is not afraid of the curve. This is a person that knows how to pace and how to get out of any situation one may find themselves in.

David knew when to run and when to rest. Rest is just as important as the wisdom of navigating. David knew how to get from point A to point B while living through the place of pain and rejection that often confronted him.

When you feel like you cannot go on, you can! If you fall, get up! You are greater than the demonic forces around you.

Question:
What are you looking at?
The setbacks or the sending forth?

— ❧ —

CHAPTER 5

Why This and Why Now?

Have you ever wondered why this, why me, and why now? These are good questions to ask yourself. Surely David ponder the same questions. Considering all the challenges David faced in his lifetime, I am sure of one thing, David's anchor was in the Lord our God.

The enemy will make sure there is an opportunity for you to step outside of God's will for you to destroy the God-given potential He has set for your life. Remember, the serpent told Eve to eat from the Tree of Knowledge of good and evil. Eve handed picked the fruit from the tree, ate of it, and shared it with Adam. Make sure you watch out for hidden traps and always remember while under attack, the battle is not yours, it belongs to the Lord. You need to recognize the source of the attack. When you know where the attack is coming from, then you will know how to respond properly.

It does not make sense when you have to pause or stop in the midst of a situation. It may not make sense to you now, but sometimes, the pause or stop is there to allow you to see what you need to see before you get to where you are going. Life is full of mysteries, you will not understand everything that comes your way. But when you walk in the truth of what the Word of God says, you will know how to handle them.

1. In Samuel 24:4–7, look at David's response and how he handled it.

   "Now's your opportunity!" David's men whispered to him. "Today the Lord is telling you, 'I will certainly put your enemy into your power to do with as you wish.'" So David crept forward and cut off a piece of the hem of Saul's robe. But then David's conscience began bothering him because he had cut Saul's robe. "The Lord knows I shouldn't have done that to my Lord the King," he said to his men. "The Lord forbid that I should do this to my Lord the king and attack the Lord's anointed one, for the Lord Himself has chosen him." So David restrained his men and did not let them kill Saul.

What seems right is not always the right thing to do. Here we see David a man whose heart is broken into pieces because his king wants him dead.

The broken pieces of David's heart was tested. In the end, David did the right thing: he spared Saul's life. We have to have the capability of putting the broken pieces of our lives in their proper place. For us to do this, we have to know and understand where those pieces belong. Some may challenge this statement, but looking through the life of David, you will see how David took the broken pieces and made them whole through his strong relationship with God. The places in his heart that was broken are now healed and made whole again.

It is easy to take pleasure in the broken pieces of our lives, especially when you have been wronged by the hand of others. How quickly we say, "See what happened to me or look at what they did." We need to remind ourselves of Romans 12:19, God says, "Vengeance is mine, I will repay."

2. David had several incidents in his life where he could have said, "Why this and why me?" After the death of Samuel which David was still in the wilderness, he had an encounter with Nabal. David sought help from Nabal for provisions for his men but Nabal refused David's request. David was angry. In David's attempt to address Nabal, Nabal's wife, Abigail, learns of the matter and intercede on behalf of her husband.

David didn't need any more distractions while in the wilderness. Yet while in wilderness on the run from Saul, there it was, his men in need of provisions. If you are facing a hurt or disappointment at the hands of someone you have been generous to, stop and evaluate the matter. Ask God for revelation of all who are involved and their role in the matter, then you will be able to take the next step in accordance to God's will and purpose. Do not allow anger or disappointment stop you from taking your next step.

1 Samuel 25 reveals Abigail's intervention in this matter. Abigail's wisdom kept David from carrying our God's role. Never forget while on the way to your destiny, you will run into opposition. Opposition can lead you to a place of discouragement if you open that door. When Abigail learned of Nabal's response to David, she immediately took actions. When she greeted David, she acknowledged who he is and who God is in David's life. Abigail's words to David calm his spirit from a place of anger to a place of peace. You see, this was not David's battle to fight. Listen carefully to what David said in 1 Samuel 25:32–35 (NLT), "David replied to Abigail, Praise the Lord, the God of Israel, who has sent you to meet me today! Bless you from keeping me from murder and from carrying out vengeance with my own hands. For I swear by the Lord, the God of Israel, who has kept me from hurting you, that if you had not hurried out to meet me, not one of Nabal's men would still be alive tomorrow morning. Then David accepted her present and told her. "Return home in peace. I have heard what you said, we will not kill your husband."

All of us have some type of behaviors and ungodliness operating in our lives that's working against us to destroy God's desire for our lives. No matter how great our failures or hurts may be, if we will continue to walk in the Spirit of God, it will lead us on a pathway of healing and restoration.

Though David had weapons and the skills to defeat giants in his life, it wasn't the weapons or his skills, it was David's attitude and response to each situation he faced.

David knew by trusting and obeying God that there was no obstacle before him that he could not defeat. There are times in our lives when why this and why me brings forth blessings in our lives. While at the lowest point in our lives, God always has a ram in the bush. Here you find David in the cave of Adullam, a place of escape from Saul. David brothers and all of his father's house heard of David's whereabouts and they went to him. And about four hundred men who also went, men who was in distress, discontented, and in debt. You can see the hand of God in this. Normally, when individuals are in distress, they focus on their own circumstance. This was ordained by God. Everyone knew David was King Saul armor bearer, now David on run from the King. Yet they went to David, to walk with him, to serve and honor what God is about to reveal through his life. We do not know how God forms his army around us but they are there. David did not seek them, they sought David. When it seems like the enemy has you surround, God has His army all around you, you are covered. So be ready! You are stronger than you think you are.

Question:
Are you ready to stand and face what God has prepared for you?

CHAPTER 6

The Ultimate Test

Let's start this chapter with a question. What will you do when the one you love betrays you?

It does not matter who you are, your faithfulness to God will be tested. Adam was tested in the Garden of Eden. Abraham was tested on a mountain in Moriah. Jesus was tested in the Garden of Gethsemane, you will be tested. Always remember to look and see where you are going in your time of testing. Location, location, location determines your place of destination. The key for your survival is stay in the river of God. Flowing in His Presence, He will always lead to a place of safety.

With everything David walked through, God was preparing him for the ultimate test…the betrayal of his beloved son Absalom. Examine your placed of preparation, it comes at various times of our lives. We are either getting ready for something, waiting on something or we are in a place of testing. Wherever you may find yourself, know that God has blessed you with weapons that will strengthen you for the journey. If you mishandle them, the enemy can and will use them against you. Forgiveness is a weapon God has given to us to fight against the attacks of the enemy. This tool is important for our lives, we need to use it. It will guide you into a perfect landing in God's arms. Yes, the landing is perfect. Getting started and staying the course can sometimes be difficult. If you maintain the attitude of walking in forgiveness, it will take you to a place in God that brings a freedom of peace and joy as you rest in God's arms. When we are in the arms of God, nothing can harm us. Walking in the fullness of forgiveness enables you to see and demonstrate God's perfect love to others no matter what they do. When you truly understand God's love, you can see a bright picture even when the picture is dark and gloomy. Jesus said in Matthew 6:14–15 (NLT), "If you forgive those who sin against you, your heavenly Father will forgive you. But if you refuse to forgive others, your Father will not forgive your sins. Walk in forgiveness, it will release you to go forth in life to a path of blessings and not curses." As long as you refuse to forgive, you will remain stuck in the past. You will not be able to move on even if you wanted too. The enemy will continue to harass you with the pain of the past, with questions such as: What happened? Who did it? And most of all, why me? You need to recognize everything that has happened to you, happened for a reason. I know this is hard to accept but it is true. Nothing can happen to you that has not filtered through the hands of God. Once you learn the ways of God, you will be able to say like Jesus said, "Not my will but Your will be done." Allowing God's will to be done in your life is what we called a yielded vessel. There are a lot of things we will not understand here on earth, but if you trust God, you can trust His handling in the matter. If you need to cry through the pain, cry. If you need to mourn, mourn but only mourn for a season. God told Joshua, "Moses my servant is dead." This was hard for Joshua and the children of Israel to accept. Moses, their leader, was no longer there to lead them. They felt helpless, their hearts mourned for their leader. God told Joshua, "Now it is your turn…arise, go." Letting go enables us to move from one thing to another.

At this point in David's life, Samuel, Jonathan, and Saul are now dead. Each one of them played a vital role in David's life. What will you do when the people that are key to your life's journey are no longer there?

David loved Saul, but Saul never found it in his heart to receive David's love. Saul's heart was full of envy, jealousy, and strife toward David. Saul allowed evil to rule his heart, causing him to be unable to govern what was in his hand. If your heart is full of strife and bitterness, then your hands will carry out what's in your heart.

David, the king of Israel, mighty man of war is about to face a challenge greater than the challenge he faced with Saul. Now it is no longer Saul but Absalom who has David on the run for his life. Although David won many battles, because of the sin David committed against Uriah, it open doors of pain for David, especially with his children, Amnon, Tamar, and Absalom.

In every situation, you need to be mindful of what you are holding in your heart. What you are holding in heart will flow to your hands. This is like the blood flowing through your body…what's in the heart will flow to your hands. If your heart is clean, your hands will remain clean. No matter what comes your way, you have to be determined that you will faithfully serve God. Have the confident in knowing that when you allow God to handle it, everything will work out for your good. Absalom made the decision to take matters in his own hands when his brother Amnon raped their sister Tamar. Absalom would not let go of the anger he held in his heart toward Amnon. This anger gripped Absalom's heart for two years. It did not stop there. Anger caused Absalom to order his brother's death for raping their sister. The enemy of our soul will do anything to destroy the purpose of God for our lives when we leave doors of bitterness and hatred in our hearts.

The open doors of bitterness will continue to work in you until you release that that has caused you pain unto the Lord. Failure to address these areas of pain will lead you down roads of hurt and disappointments. There are many roads you will travel on before you get to where God has appointed for you. Jesus understood this. You see, many people questioned Jesus's authority. Who are you? Why are you doing what you are doing? But Jesus knew who He was and what our Heavenly Father called Him to do. Even when you run into bumps along the way, make sure your foundation is strong and solid. While in the Garden of Gethsemane, Jesus faced much agony. Life will sometimes make you feel like you cannot conquer this mountain, but you can! You need to rest and know that God is in control and not you. Apart from God, you can do nothing but with God all things are possible to him that believe. Jesus made a powerful statement in Matthew 26:42 (NLT), "My Father! If this cup cannot be taken away unless I drink it, your will be done." Never focus on what you are facing, place your focus on God. Read His Word, the Holy Bible and believe and trust in His Word. If Jesus faced agony and oppression, be assured you will too. What did Jesus do? He got up! What do you need to do? Get up and face this mountain that is before you and stand in the place God has called and prepared just for you.

Now after the murder of Amnon, Absalom flees to his grandfather. He stayed there for three years. He manipulates Joab, David's servant into seeking his father's permission to return home. Permission is granted, Absalom returns home to Jerusalem but not to his father's (the king's) table. This insults Absalom. Absalom sets out to steal the hearts of the people of Israel, and he did.

It was not enough that David granted Absalom permission to return home after plotting and ordering his brother's death. Absalom wanted to be at his father's table. Be careful with the key you are holding in your hand. What is it unlocking?

Years later, Absalom still has not addressed the issues in his heart toward his father. Absalom thinks he has stolen his father's prize possession, the people of Israel. He sets out to destroy his father. When David receives word of this, he flees. While on the run from Absalom, David learns of many acts of betrayal against him. David was cursed at, stones thrown at him and his men. He was accused of stealing Saul's throne. Even though we know Saul was dethrone by God and not David, David is accused of something he did not do. Does this sound familiar? Several times on my journey, I was accused of things I did not do. If you find yourself in this position, trust God. Trust Him and know that things will work out for your good. This is a hard place to be in, but you need to stay the course and know that God is on your side. Keep going; David did and so can you. He did not quit nor did he give up.

Once again, David was running for his life. You may be tired and weary but do not quit. You may think it but do not speak it. Words are powerful. Listen to what God is saying and not what your emotions are saying to you. Your emotions will play tricks on you. One minute you are up, and the next minute your feel like a failure. It is dangerous to make a decision out of your emotions. Know the importance of staying faithful to God's Word. Isaiah 40:31 says, "Those who wait on the Lord shall renew their strength, they shall mount up with wings like eagles, they shall run and not be weary, they shall walk and not faint." You need to know that no matter what is chasing you, God has your back covered. He is behind you with each step you take. He is your rear guard. David knew nothing could happen to him unless it went through the hands of God. When Shimei, a servant, also a member of Saul's household cursed David, David's men wanted to retaliate. David responded from his heart and not his emotions, "If the Lord has told him (Shimei) to curse me, who are you to stop him?" David also said, "And perhaps the Lord will see that I am being wronged and will bless me because of these curses today" (2 Samuel 16).

Of all the things David encountered, he never thought he would encounter the betrayal of his son, but he did.

What will you do when the evil intends of someone's heart is revealed to you? When David learned of Absalom's whereabouts, he ordered his soldiers to apprehend Absalom but do not kill him. In the end, it was Absalom who was dead and not David. David's men who stood by him was ashamed because of David's response to Absalom's death. David was encouraged to acknowledge the faithfulness of his soldiers and what they did on the battlefield to protect their king from the murdering hands of Absalom.

At the beginning and end of every battle, there are decisions to be made. Which direction will you take? What will you do when the dust has settled? After Absalom sought revenge against Amnon, he failed to seek God's guidance for healing and restoration. Instead, he chose the path of destruction. He did not know how to let go and allow God to settle the matter. He never learned the art of forgiveness while living with his father. It was not the fact that David ignored what Amnon did to Tamar, it was David's understanding of what forgiveness mean. Forgiveness does not look at what a person has done, it causes you to look at your role in response to what happened. You are not responsible for the actions of others, but you are responsible for your actions.

David reconciled that his ultimate test was not Absalom and what Absalom did to him, but his ultimate test was he needed to move on. Stepping out of the place he was in, moving to the place that was prepared for him. If only Absalom would have recognized this earlier in his life. If this is a place of pain for you, take a moment now and pray. Ask God to pierce the darkness in your heart so that you are free from the pain that has caused you so much heartache and disappointment. Make a decision now that you will live a life free from all the guilt and shame of a wrong done to you to a life filled with the joy and strength that will allow you to conquer your dreams of hope. Our Lord is there, He is able to do what you cannot do. His strength is prefect in our times of weakness.

At the end of this event in David's life, he found himself in a position he thought he would not be in. The son he loved is dead. David made a decision; he released the matter and moved on. Never allow the death of someone or something in your life blind your vision for the future.

Question:
What are you holding?

CHAPTER 7

The Lord Is My Shepherd

After all the things David faced from the beginning to the end, David's declaration in Psalm 23 will stand forever. As you read Psalm 23, read it as though you never read it before. Allow God's word to become alive in a way that you have never heard it before. It is life. It is medicine for those in need. Are you in need today of a Savior? One who can do what no man can do. I pray that His word will restore every broken pieces in your life and bring you to a place in Him that will enable to walk, run, and stand in the anointing of His power for your life. Read and listen with a commitment heart.

> The Lord is my shepherd, I shall not want
> He maketh me to lie down in green pastures, He leadeth me beside the still waters.
> He restoreth my soul, He leadeth me in the paths of righteousness for His name's sake.
> Yea though I walk through the valley of the shadow of death. I will fear no evil: for Thou are with me; Thy rod and Thy staff they comfort me.
> Thou preparest a table before me in the presence of mine enemies:
> Thou anointest my head with oil; my cup runneth over.
> Surely goodness and mercy shall follow me all the days of my life: I will dwell in the house of the Lord forever.

The Message Bible says, "God, is my Shepherd! I don't need a thing." Because David faithfully acknowledged God as the one that lead him, David was not afraid of no man. Even though David ran from Saul, he was not afraid of Saul. David feared the anointing of God and not the man. David respected Saul and his authority, David never lost sight of God's purpose. David tried his best to demonstrate his love for Saul, but Saul could not receive it. David knew he was a gifted man and what he was called to do.

David revealed to us how he trust in the Lord for protection in Psalm 11:1. How the God he served delivered him from the hands of Saul, from the paw of lions and bears, is the same God who kept him. When someone wronged you and you know for a fact that they did, leave it in the hands of God. Never take the matter into your hands.

David, a strong warrior in battle, he knew that the weapons in his hands were not greater than the matter in God's heart. It was never God's will for David to kill Saul and then become king. This is not how God operates. As a believer, ask God, "Am I handling this the way you want or am I doing things my way?" One of the greatest examples of a survival is when we let go and allow God to fight our battles. Jesus reveals this to us in John 10:17–18, "Therefore My Father loves Me, because I lay down My life that I may take it again. No one takes it from Me, but I lay it down of Myself. I have the power to lay it down, and I have power to take it again. This command I have received from My Father."

Do you know where to go for life support? David did. God knows you will survive this! Do you? David knew he was a survivor because of who walked with him, God Almighty, the God of his fathers, Abraham, Isaac, and Jacob.

As David's life draws close to the end, I love what he said to Solomon, his son, in 1 Kings 2:2 (NLT), "I am going where everyone on earth must someday go. Take courage and be a man." David knew his work here on earth was finished. He instructs Solomon of the things he should do and never forget to observe the requirements of the Lord. What a teachable moment. What lives are you changing? Are the things you teach leading someone to God's way of doing things or to your way? When the Lord is your Shepherd, you will always lead people to Him.

The sword in David's hand never forced out the fire in his heart to serve God. Why? Because David kept his hands in God's hands. Studying the life of David will encourage you through any storms of life. It will guide you even when you are sailing in the wrong direction. David asked God to lead him, make his way plain for him to follow God. Because he knew that no matter where God was taking him, he was not alone. When the Lord is your Shepherd, you know Him as your shield, your shelter, the only One who can and who will deliver you!

For you alone oh God is my Rock, my sword and shield. The One I can lean on in good and bad times. My only source of strength in times of trouble. My faithful God.

Question:
Who or what is leading you?

Here are scriptures that helped me along my journey. May they richly bless and strengthen you as you walk with the Lord our God.

> Oh, fear the Lord, you His saints! There is no want to those who fear Him. The young lions lack and suffer hunger; but those who seek the Lord shall not lack any good thing. (Psalm 34:9–10)

> Call upon Me in the day of trouble, I will deliver you, and you shall glorify Me. (Psalm 50:14)

> Cast your burden on the Lord, and He shall sustain you; He shall never permit the righteous to be moved. (Psalm 55:22)

> In God I have put my trust, I will not be afraid. What can man do to me? (Psalm 56:11)

> For the Lord God is a sun and shield. The Lord
> will give grace and glory; no good thing will
> he withhold from those who walk uprightly.
> (Psalm 84:11)

Trust in the Lord. He will guide you, protect you, and shield you. His word is faithful and true. Allow the Lord to lead you every step of the way. Heaven and earth will pass away, but the Word of God remains forever and ever! Allow Jesus to govern your heart.

> Jesus said, "I am the way, the truth and the life,
> no one comes to the Father except through Me."
> (John 14:6)

Jesus is knocking at your door, open it, He is there for you, Jesus Christ is Lord!

The main part of David's life revealed the power of God's anointing in his life. David fought battle after battles, challenge after challenges, yet he remained faithful to his God and to the cause that was assigned to him. Remember, God is always with you. He will see you through as a victor and not a victim. Absolutely nothing can defeat you when you channel all not some but all of life's obstacles through God. God is the only one who can deliver you! How you see the storms of life is how you see your God, Jehovah God, the great I Am, the God of Abraham, Isaac and Jacob...so why not you?

Why not you being the one God has called to walk through whatever you are facing for such a time as this. A time that will bring glory and honor to His name as you walk through life being an example of our Lord and Savior Jesus Christ. Jesus did and so can you!

ABOUT THE AUTHOR

Cynthia Paul Finklea is a part of the pastoral and elder staff at Lamb's Chapel Christian Center. She also serves as part of the intercessory prayer team. Cynthia and her husband, Herman, under the leadership of their pastor, oversee the Nehemiah Ministry, assisting those in need. Cynthia graduated from Cathedral Bible College in May 1997 with an associate's degree in theology. She is married to her husband for thirty-nine years. They enjoy laughing together and celebrating life as God has purposed. They served on mission trips to Nicaragua and Kenya. Her heart's desire is to be faithful to what God has called her to do and to love His people.